4

SHOULD OUR UNDOING COME DOWN UPON US WHITE

Winner of the 2013 Frost Place Chapbook Competition

should
our undoing
come down
upon us
white

POEMS BY JILL OSIER

BULL★CITY
PRESS

DURHAM, NORTH CAROLINA

SHOULD OUR UNDOING
COME DOWN UPON US WHITE

Frost Place Chapbook Competition Judge for 2013: Patrick Donnelly

Published in the United States of America

Library of Congress Cataloging-in-Publication Data

Osier, Jill
Should Our Undoing Come Down Upon Us White: poems / by Jill Osier
p. cm.
ISBN-13: 978-1-4243-1801-8 (Paperback)

Cover painting by Marina Mariya
Book design by Flying Hand Studio

Published by Bull City Press
1217 Odyssey Drive
Durham, NC 27713
http://bullcitypress.com

ACKNOWLEDGEMENTS

THE ADIRONDACK REVIEW
Flame

ARTS & LETTERS
The Snow Is Almost Again Mended
This Close

COPPER NICKEL
Left to Itself the Heart Mistakes Snow

CRAB CREEK REVIEW
Someday My Stomach Will Be a Museum

THE GETTYSBURG REVIEW
Second Sky
Spring Has Such Tiny Wrists

GREEN MOUNTAINS REVIEW
The Sea of Too Far Is Unmapped

THE GREENSBORO REVIEW
To Have Been on Fire

PASSAGES NORTH
Last Dream of Flowers

POETRY
Left to Itself the Heart Could Almost Melt, Mend
Should Our Undoing Come Down Upon Us White
Snow Becoming Light by Morning

PRAIRIE SCHOONER
Floodwater
Obscura
Thaw

VERSAL
Proof
Winter Song

CONTENTS

and should we stand with arms outstretched for a refrain

THE SEA OF TOO FAR IS UNMAPPED

Maybe this is the night.

The night that can finally take the shape, though not the sound, maybe never the sound, of the story of a man who loses his knife while cleaning the goose he shot from a canoe he's been paddling for weeks, alone, far from anyone.

This man could love a woman, and this woman could be miles away, she could be dying. And in fact he does, and she is, and she is.

Tonight inside me a space without sound, or any amount of understanding, is reserved for just this.

The story is not about loss, or what fails to rise to the surface.
It is not about last breath.

But I cannot wear red, after the small bird came and circled the time she cut his hair, circling—snip—pausing, scissors still, to remember the shape of his head, snip, the skin of his neck, snip. Red bird circling.

I will tell all of it someday—the knife, the canoe, the red bird—I can say to a lover, but I don't know. Where would I go then?

LEFT TO ITSELF THE HEART COULD ALMOST MELT, MEND

When the Amish girl gets off the bus
she walks over and stomps
her small black boot into a drift
in front of McDonald's.
She is maybe new to winter
this far north and wants to know
its depth. Its give. Oh,
be careful. It already has you
by the night of your dress,
violet-black with white-dotted print.

WINTER SONG

Today I came from a meadow's snow, past tree wells, their low
bellies warm, past deer beds, empty, to blacktop. I shouldn't be
surprised by roads, but this one came on and held the hillside
like a dark band of fat. When the first car passed, all of last
night's stars fell quietly from my pocket. Fiddler, are you
coming home? The bird I've kept behind my back,
could I hold it up for you, would be the size of the sun.

SECOND SKY

The father works to make a second sky
for his children, in case the first one
runs out or proves false. In case its
loveliness leaves it vulnerable, like
a collarbone. If you go far enough
north, just before the trees give way,
just as the air you breathe takes on
rough edges, you'll see him who lives
on a mountain, who from his frozen
dome has learned there are no secrets
to ice. Nor are there substitutes,
nor excuses. It is a matter of muscle
and time, his and the ice's, before
the second sky, a shineless, dead-colored
compass floating in a peace of snow,
is finished. His children have watched
him work, not knowing how he hoped
they were watching the ice, so they might
know which sky was which, though
children, he remembers, only see
one sky. Already they spin
and miss each other's hands,
unaware of how their hearts align.

SHOULD OUR UNDOING COME DOWN UPON US WHITE

Even while we talked, snow must have been falling. Now it's a scar:
I've mostly failed in the rooms

of honesty and forthrightness. Let me
explain. A child says, *Stand anywhere you want*

right here. I watch her sled. Orange plastic, busted,
duct-taped in two places, it barely waits for her

before shooting the steep drive. At four,
she is all snot, bangs, and spunk. She plods and sculpts.

After many tries, she settles into something
the sled finds true.

LEFT TO ITSELF THE HEART MISTAKES SNOW

Here it comes, with all our efforts
to stake it down, all the corners
temporary. Babe, here's

to the half-made houses, to those
unexpected slivers of light. I know
you are tired of carpentry. I know

your own roof almost killed you,
rising like the wave you fancied
it to be. Trails from here, I know

they all go down. I'll stay
despite the very best one. So when
you fashion your mid-winter horse

from plaster and its tail falls off
like ash, okay. We'll sweep it out
to the rest of the sea.

SOMEDAY MY STOMACH WILL BE A MUSEUM

Everything here eats.
Ki from next door, a snowsuit in pigtails,
clomps in hungry. The half tortilla she finds
hides half her face, her mouth, which says
she runs from boys who are funny.
I ask why, and the tortilla says
she doesn't run from girls who are funny.
I ask why, and the tortilla says she runs
from a particular boy who is funny because
he hurts her. She jumps from couch
to chair to couch while I do dishes,
hauling snowbroth from the stove.
When she's called home, I stand and watch
the dark take her. Sometimes windows
are not windows. A curtain of old cloth
hangs from the edge of the counter,
sogged along the bottom where it soaks up
what the dog spills. It hides compost
and the slop bucket. I squat down and dig out
the thumbtacks, grab the hammer and slam
extra-large nails into the fabric, shaking the walls.
When you come in, pissed because ice has swallowed
half the driveway and gnaws its way beneath the porch,
you're starving and smell of the hay bales you've put down
to stall it. I feed the fire until you're shirtless
while you cook, your shoulders
soft bitable rounds.

APOLOGY

Hauling logs to heap a box
by the stove—bark, ice,
dirt with each load—we wear
our breath, we wear
the same clothes, the same tracks
in and out while the heart's fog blows
different each day—ah, but there's
the creak from the stove, the hatchet
tamping wide the grate, your chest
blowing the flames up.

FLAME

You wish this was your long shadow.

It was once, up where the earth curves hard from the light,
you with a suitcase on a blinding sea. You stood on ice and knew

it moved beneath, like a warm-blooded creature
does in sleep.

We could have let the cold take us.

But that was the year we beat winter back, warmed by the effort. *Too bad
winter couldn't stay,* I'd say. Your heart, red wax,

slipped soft from its nail. I shaped it back, and the two of us lay waiting
in a cabin's draft.

If we close our eyes, our mouths can tell the difference better than truth:

ice is fast and unashamed, and fire stretches like an echo—do you hear it
break softly in two, like a word, like embers?

THE SNOW IS ALMOST AGAIN MENDED

If only the heart thickened as it fell.

If only it could last

the season, summon cheer

from some field—fine, yes,

you ski ahead. Oh, how you fit

the wintry scene,

cutting, quiet.

TO HAVE BEEN ON FIRE

The mind goes, eventually,
where it needs to go. As does the body.

Not so with the heart.
The heart has nothing for need. It sits in a little hut,
and all the roads are well worn, all the wagons breaking.

Tonight's breakthrough is I try to lull myself
by imagining that I have been badly burned.

In the drawings I can't draw there is a new window
open on the left side of my neck. The lulling is for this,
for shutting it.

THIS CLOSE

The trees along the river are slipping
back into their lavender cloaks
with that calm of someone in a doorway
who's already gone. Gone gray in nearby yards
are the small, free-standing sheds kids run around at dusk,
falling, trying to prolong a day that is falling
back to its simplest shapes. And closer still,
the smallest of those tiny moles gathered below
your right eye, its little patch of stars, always out, never clouded,
and you blinking, just blinking, like the horse or dog
who, patient, adored, takes it.

OBSCURA

It was a one-room cabin
still missing some windows. Starlight,

snowlight. Far from the world, far enough the dark
was true, could be its truest.

Nights we'd stand under stars streaming, sung to
by electric wires and cold.

Shaking the scene now, snow falls,
smoke rising up to meet it.

Wasn't there something
we could make once?

A small, simple box with a tiny hole
for light to come through,

make everything clearer? Didn't it work
by its smallness, its dark?

I swear. I don't know where
we would have needed to live.

PROOF

The small hole a dog
started digging in the backyard
grew. I woke one day to the whole
place excavated. A grave
for our house. I wanted to call you,
invite you to the service, but it has been
so long, the sidewalks at dusk so straight,
screen door flung like I might be
just getting clothes off the line or out
in the garden for a handful of snow.

LAST DREAM OF FLOWERS ·

"Cart" is the only word I gather through the sweaty brow and German

of a man who's out of breath, bothered, but I'm determined, eventually

hit the tavern, where folks lean, and now they're leaning in close to see

the bundle, oo-and-ah-ing, *What had the American chosen?* You're there

with noon beer and pistachios, and when I sit, the waitress—coin purse

mouthing open at her hip—squeezes the head of a dead-blue tulip, says

with thickest tongue, *You must keep these cold.*

SNOW BECOMING LIGHT BY MORNING

In case you sit across from the meteorologist tonight,
and in case the dim light over the booth in the bar still shines
almost planetary on your large, smooth, winter-softened
forehead, in case all of the day—its woods and play, its fire—
has stayed on your beard, and will stay through the slight
drift of mouth, the slackening of even your heart's muscle—
...well. I am filled with snow. There's nothing to do now
but wait.

THAW

I loved your father most
when I stole his slippers
and went to him and confessed.
He knew. I could feel it in my teeth,
my feet were that cold.

Today winter fields shine
with emptiness. Sometimes
a windmill. The barns, too, are giving up,
in patches, their last disguise.

SPRING HAS SUCH TINY WRISTS

The whitetail sometimes number

thirty in the yard. I wake and find

they're already there. At dusk

they share the hills' brown-gray,

ghosts. The locals warned me

about this time of year, the mud,

the not knowing. How it'd be winter,

then spring, then overnight winter.

It sounded okay, sounded familiar. Anyway,

all of it's quiet. This morning I watch two deer

through a veil, a snow that's become small blankets

on their backs. Soon it'll hide their hooves,

their tracks, soundless. Like a girl's breath

on a window, before it's warm enough

to break, and she will, with the others,

for the woods outside the correctional.

LITTLE TOWNS SHINING IN THE DISTANCE

When the young man on the bus crosses his leg to settle into his book, a chunk of snow slips silent from his boot. He leans to look over the edge of his seat, as if he's dropped

a coin or handkerchief. Closing the book, he swivels both feet neatly into the aisle and gently stomps them twice, checks, resumes his reading.

I have been traveling longer than him. My whole body hums,
my boots dry with nowhere.

FLOODWATER

Something left this morning after making a small river of me.
Left after the small river was made, where I make a small river.
Yesterday I tried to explain about the smell,
how it was coming up out of the ground.
Mild days to savor, to be not sure.
Days to watch for the red bird, to run wet and dull,
bright, then dull. Days to find the chickadees
helmeted and ready.

ABOUT THE AUTHOR

JILL OSIER studied poetry at Luther College and the University of Alaska Fairbanks. Her honors include a National Endowment for the Arts Fellowship, the Diane Middlebrook Poetry Fellowship, and the Campbell Corner Poetry Prize. She is the author of a chapbook, *Bedful of Nebraskas*, and lives in Fairbanks, Alaska.